Original title:
In the Shadow of Twinkling Lights

Copyright © 2024 Creative Arts Management OÜ
All rights reserved.

Author: Eleanor Prescott
ISBN HARDBACK: 978-9916-94-380-9
ISBN PAPERBACK: 978-9916-94-381-6

Reflections in a Midnight Pool

Bobbing ducks in the starry night,
Chasing moonbeams, quite a sight.
Jumping over, splashes flare,
Wondering who's holding the dare.

Frogs croak jokes with croaking glee,
Ripples carry laughs with glee.
Beware the munching fish nearby,
Eating tales of yonder sky.

Serenade of Flickering Fireflies

Tiny dancers with glowing butts,
Swinging low and making cuts.
They form a line, a twinkling train,
Winking at me, oh what a gain!

Giggles hidden in the grass,
As fireflies join in for a pass.
They flicker tunes, a sparkling fit,
While crickets play the drum, a hit!

A Night Sky's Silent Poetry

Stars scribble secrets from above,
Wishing wells and dreams we shove.
Each twinkle tells a funny tale,
Of cosmic antics, far from pale.

Clouds drift by with a dreamy sigh,
Whispering thoughts as they float high.
They trip on stars, oh what a plight,
Fumbling in the soft moonlight.

Lanterns of Reminiscence

Old lanterns sway in a gentle breeze,
Telling stories with such ease.
Memories glow, a flicker here,
Making even the stoic cheer.

Each flick brings back a joyful night,
When laughter danced with pure delight.
They hang like fruit from every post,
Pondering who we missed the most.

Hushed Chants of the Celestial Night

Stars whisper secrets, oh so light,
Dancing around in a comical flight.
Planets collide with a giggle or two,
While comets race past, chasing a shoe.

Alien frogs play leapfrog on Mars,
Trading their tales with raucous guitars.
Nebulae sparkle in laughter so bright,
As the universe joins in a delight.

Lanterns of Forgotten Wishes

Balloons float up to a moon's embrace,
Tethered to dreams in a whimsical chase.
Wishes forgotten, now tie their shoes,
Chasing after giggles, spreading good news.

Light bulbs buzz with a giggling cheer,
Mocking the starlight that winkles sincere.
Forgotten hopes dance in currents of air,
As lanterns chuckle without a care.

Murmurs Beneath the Moonlit Glow

Crickets chirp in a conga line,
While shadows gather for a little fine wine.
Under the glow of a bulbous moon,
Silly owls hoot a light-hearted tune.

Gnomes on rooftops take a daring dive,
As night blooms open, spirits arrive.
Ghosts tell jokes that crack the still night,
While shadows erupt into fits of delight.

A Tapestry of Nighttime Secrets

Mice make mischief on the garden fence,
Plotting their pranks with a touch of suspense.
Bats overhead trade their flight for a dance,
While sleepy flowers join the night's romance.

Fireflies glow with a twinkle and tease,
Flirting with dreams on a playful breeze.
In this canvas of laughter and thrill,
Naught but joy spreads across the hill.

Twilight's Sotto Voce

Beneath the stars, my cat does dance,
In moonlit shadows, he takes a chance.
Whiskers twitching, a nose so bold,
He pounces at dusk, adventures untold.

Laughter spills from the boughs above,
The chirps of crickets, they play and shove.
A clever owl with a wink and a grin,
Says, 'What's more funny, the twilight or sin?'

Flickering Memories in the Night

The fireflies blink like tiny fools,
Trying to rally, breaking all the rules.
One zips past my nose, oh what a sight,
I swat and I giggle, it's quite the fright!

Old stories come back as the night wears thin,
Of ghosts that dance, and stubborn gin.
With each flicker they bring to delight,
Memories spark like a candlelight.

Luminous Trails of the Heart

Silly stars twinkle like sparkly snaps,
They giggle and wink from their cosmic laps.
A comet races by, full of sass,
'Hold on to your hats,' it says with a laugh.

In the dark, we chase our silly dreams,
Painting the night with our luminous beams.
With laughter shared in the gleaming air,
We find our joy, floating without a care.

Riddles Written in Light Dust

What's that sparkle? A question of fate,
A riddle of light, we ponder and wait.
The stars above seem to giggle and tease,
Whispers of wonders carried by the breeze.

With a wink, the night steals our sleep,
As shadows gather in piles, all neat.
A treasure of laughter laid out to dive,
In this midnight jest, we feel so alive.

Glows of Solitude at Midnight

The fridge hums softly, a midnight friend,
It's there for laughter, snacks that never end.
Under the flicker of the single bulb,
I dance like nobody, my moves quite a jolt.

Shadows peek in, they glimpse at my show,
Chairs join in, they sway to and fro.
A cat looks puzzled, judging my styles,
As I trip on my socks and spin with big smiles.

Beneath the Glittering Canopy

The stars play hide and seek in the night,
While I chase fireflies, feeling quite bright.
Giggles erupt as I trip on my feet,
The night takes my dreams and makes them a treat.

Bugs join the chorus, a buzzing refrain,
They march through the air like they've lost their brain.
For every twinkle, a laugh's floating high,
In this starry mess, I'm the just-from-the-cry.

The Quiet Symphony of Stars

The crickets are tuning their night-time song,
I think they're off-key, it's going quite wrong.
A lone owl hoots; is he laughing at me?
Or is he just pondering the night's jubilee?

A comet zooms past, with a tail oh so bright,
I swear it just winked as I danced with delight.
Each star seems to giggle, a heavenly band,
As I wave my arms like a mad marionette hand.

A Tapestry of Night's Embrace

The moon plays peek-a-boo behind the trees,
While I whisper secrets to the wandering breeze.
Fluffy clouds join in, all drifting along,
Competing with me in this dance-off so wrong.

I trip on the grass, pretending to glide,
A bouquet of laughter blooms far and wide.
Each stumble a note in this playful spree,
A symphony of awkward, just night and me.

Whispers of the City Lights

The neon signs giggle, what a sight,
While pigeons strut in humorous flight.
A streetlamp winks with a fluorescent grin,
As late-night pizza folks dive right in.

Taxi horns play a chaotic song,
While the lost tourists wander along.
Street performers juggle, but drop their props,
And laughter erupts, oh how it hops!

The moon's a jester, casting bright beams,
Reflecting on dreamers and their wild dreams.
With every chuckle, the stars align,
In this city where the funny meets the divine.

So here we roam, with a heart full of glee,
Under lights that whisper, just let it be.
Each corner we turn, there's something to see,
A comedic tale of urban jubilee.

Illusions of the Illuminated Night

The disco ball spins like a spinning top,
Reflecting antics from a city non-stop.
A dog in a tutu struts down the lane,
As laughter echoes, it's never mundane.

Bistro tables host a clumsy affair,
Where a couple spills wine, without a care.
Waiters glide by, like they own a stage,
Turning every mishap into a new page.

A saxophonist plays off-key tunes,
While lovers serenade under cartoon moons.
The street art giggles, as it comes alive,
In this silly place where dreams survive.

With twinkling colors, it's all in fun,
This nightly adventure just begun.
With chuckles and winks, we dance through the bright,
Lost in the charm of this illuminated night.

Journey Through Celestial Reflections

Stars are laugh tracks in the sky so wide,
As we navigate the streets with comical pride.
Sidewalk cafes overflow with delight,
Cappuccinos spill on a very short knight.

Balloons float high, just out of reach,
While kids chase their dreams, it's a funny speech.
The city hums like a jazz band gone wild,
Unexpected giggles from every child.

Night carts serve food, oh what a sight,
With pickles and fries, a glorious bite.
The moon's a chef, preparing a feast,
As we dance through the chaos, never ceased.

So let's embark on this whimsical ride,
With joy and laughter, always as our guide.
In the glow of the night, we find our groove,
In this playful dance, let's all just move.

Secrets of the Midnight Carnival

Underneath the vibrant tents,
Clowns juggle, and laughter bends.
Popcorn flies, a sweetened breeze,
As llamas dance with utmost ease.

The fortune teller spills hot tea,
Sipping secrets, wild and free.
A unicycle chase around the chair,
With rubber chickens everywhere!

Balloon animals float and sway,
While tightrope walkers steal the day.
A magician's trick, a rebel yell,
Turns kittens into fish that smell!

The moon laughs at every prank,
As jugglers leap from cozy plank.
Cotton candy clouds of fluff,
Who knew midnight could be so tough?

Shimmering Dreams in Urban Spaces

City buzz, graffiti storms,
Neon lights wear crazy forms.
Socks and flip-flops stroll the street,
As squirrels plan their dance-off feat.

A hot dog rolls in tender pride,
While pigeons practice synchronized glide.
Street art speaks in whispers bold,
Of dreams that sparkle, bright and gold.

Buses honk a silly tune,
Street performers dance 'neath the moon.
A banjo strums the city's heart,
As taxis fly like work of art!

Each corner hides a playful show,
With sprightly laughs and curvy flow.
A skyline stitched with laughter bold,
In urban dreams, no one grows old!

Nights Wrapped in Radiant Veils

Twinkling fabrics drape the scene,
Ghosts in taffeta all serene.
A disco ball spins tales of cheer,
While jellybeans burst and disappear.

Hats that dance upon their heads,
Penguins strut in shiny threads.
The music hums a giggly song,
As jellyfish sway all night long.

Under the sparkly canopy,
Goblins giggle, wild and free.
A bubble machine in full swing,
Makes each laugh a shiny thing.

Each moment wraps in laughing light,
As the stars decide to join the night.
In this circus of delight,
Funny magic takes its flight!

Silhouettes in a Sea of Light

Starlit shadows prance and play,
In an alley where cats don't stay.
The moon wears a goofy grin,
While nocturnal squirrels sneak in.

A lamplight flickers, almost sways,
As crickets hold their dance parades.
Mirrors reflect a one-eyed dog,
In a fancy, fluffy fog.

The night skies throw a shadow show,
Where hummingbirds dip down low.
Ghosts play tag with flying kites,
In this haven of giggly nights.

Each corner hums a funny tune,
As stars twinkle like cartoon.
In the glow of wit and beam,
Silhouettes dance, a joyful dream!

Secrets of the Urban Glow

City lights flicker, folks get wild,
Beneath the gleam, the street dogs smiled.
Neon signs wink, the taxis race,
While pigeons strut, they own the place.

Laughter echoes, shadows prance,
Mice in tuxedos join the dance.
Hot dogs sizzle, aroma so bright,
As ketchup fights with mustard's bite.

Under the glow, the odd friends meet,
A squirrel in shades, a raccoon with feet.
They gossip tales of the late-night scene,
And steal the fries, you know what I mean!

In the bright of night, all bets are off,
A cat on a skateboard starts to scoff.
With urban lore and quirky flair,
The glow reveals a silly affair.

Dances of Distant Fireflies

Tiny lights twirl in the dusk's embrace,
Fireflies tango in a bug ballet space.
They mock the stars with a glorious blink,
While crickets compose a tune to sink.

Grass blades whisper, gossip on the scene,
As ants march in lines, proud and keen.
Bugs in tuxedos tap on the ground,
Turning the night into festival sound.

A moth flutters by with a grand debut,
Waving to friends in the shimmering queue.
With glowing butts, they spark a sight,
And dance till dawn, oh what a night!

In the moon's soft glow, they shine like gems,
Plotting escapes from the world's rams.
Under the smiles of dainty light,
Bug parties thrive in the calm of night.

Reflections on a Luminous Canvas

Canvas wide with luminescent cheer,
Streaks of neon spill, oh so near.
A dog in shades gets its portrait drawn,
Wagging its tail at the break of dawn.

Splash of colors, splattered in jest,
A clown juggles beer cans, doing his best.
Rubber ducks float in the puddles bright,
As laughter erupts in the cool night light.

From alleys glow a mystery tour,
A pizza slice spins, looking for more.
In the laughter's hue, faces aglow,
Painted with joy, where wild dreams flow.

And as the evening unwinds its show,
Reflections giggle, dance, and grow.
Each corner whispers a tale of delight,
In this colorful world, full of light.

Illumination's Quiet Whisper

Where street lamps hum their mellow tune,
A raccoon strums a garbage can boon.
With a wink and a nod, they steal the scene,
While shadows giggle, so carefree and keen.

The moon rolls by, a spectator sly,
As a hedgehog attempts to jump high.
Bounding along on mischief's quest,
In the quiet glow, they're truly blessed.

Parks become stages under the night,
With owls in spectacles and hearts full of light.
A strut here, a flap there, all in good fun,
Illumination's nightly race just begun.

With secrets shared in the flickering beams,
Life's silly moments flow like dreams.
As laughter swirls and the night takes a bow,
The dance goes on, here and now.

A Symphony of Glow and Gloom

Beneath the glow of neon bright,
The pigeons dance without a fright.
A hotdog rolls, a mustard spill,
While laughter echoes, time stands still.

Cats in hats and dogs that prance,
Join the late-night salsa dance.
With every honk and playful cheer,
The city sings, so full of cheer.

But faintly creeping through the fun,
Are shadows lurking, on the run.
A light bulb flickers, a fleeting jest,
As we all wait for the morning quest.

So raise a cup to night's delight,
For every giggle that feels just right.
In this vibrant, silly, gleaming maze,
We'll find our joy in nighttime's haze.

Veils of City Light

The traffic twirls like a cheap ballet,
Where taxis race, come what may.
Here comes a bus, it missed its stop,
As if the rules just let them drop.

Squirrels dart across the road,
A spice of chaos in this abode.
In every alley, a rumor flies,
Of pizza slices and late-night pies.

Flashy signs whisper sweet temptation,
While street performers seek ovation.
A juggling clown, a mime that sighs,
All woven through with twinkly lies.

Yet laughter bubbles, an urban thrill,
Through every corner and every hill.
As dreams collide beneath the beams,
We chase the night with silly schemes.

The Beauty of Cosmic Shadows

The stars above, a chandelier,
While down below, we toast with beer.
A couple hugs, a taxi sways,
In this cosmic dance, life displays.

A glowing moon, a cake of cheese,
As parties spill in evening breeze.
We spin with glee, trip on the curb,
Just city folk without a blurb.

The beauty lies in jolly faces,
Fumbling feet and quirky places.
With each adventure, a tale to tell,
Of funny moments where we fell.

So here's to nights that make us bold,
With dreams and stories still untold.
We'll drift in joy, let laughter soar,
In cosmic shadows, forevermore.

Echoing Stars in Silent Streets

On quiet streets, we skip and hop,
Chasing echoes, we just can't stop.
A cat in boots, a squirrel with flair,
In our glowing world, there's magic to share.

Bikes that wobble and laughter loud,
As we weave through the midnight crowd.
With every giggle, a twinkling light,
We dance like stars, a pure delight.

Through alleyways and sidestreets deep,
We stumble over dreams in our sleep.
A hero wave from passing cars,
This merry chaos, our sparkling stars.

So raise a toast to silly charms,
To city life and all its harms.
For in this journey, wild and free,
We find our joy just you and me.

Dappled Light Beneath the Canopy

Underneath the boughs so wide,
The fireflies begin to glide.
They dance around like tiny sprites,
Winging it under moonlit nights.

A squirrel steals a lover's fries,
While owls hoot their wise goodbyes.
The shadows play a silly game,
While critters share their tales of fame.

A raccoon lost in his own head,
Rummaging for a piece of bread.
We giggle as he takes a dive,
In the light, he feels alive.

So here we sit with snacks in tow,
Enjoying nature's funny show.
With laughter bright and spirits high,
Beneath the trees, we dream and sigh.

The Enchantment of Urban Illumination

City lights, they flash and sway,
Bouncing high in vibrant play.
The streetlamps wink, a secret share,
While pigeons find their style to flare.

In the park a jogger trips,
Stumbling past, he gives us quips.
With neon signs that boldly sing,
Our laughter's loud, like springtime's fling.

A cat walks proud, in shades of sass,
Ignoring all who dare to pass.
Yet every beam that fills the street
Makes chaos dance — oh, what a treat!

So let's embrace this glowing night,
Where every turn is sheer delight.
A starry laugh in roofless skies,
In this bright maze, our spirits rise.

Glimmers of Hope in the Dark

In the corner, a glint we see,
A lost sock's brighter than can be.
It twinkles like a distant star,
Just wishing it was not so far.

But wait! A moth, in fierce pursuit,
Thinks that it's a nectar fruit.
He flaps and flops, a silly sight,
While critters laugh, oh what a night!

A flash from phones, a selfie craze,
We strike a pose in funky ways.
The darkness fades with every snap,
Creating laughter's sweetest map.

So let the night bring joy to us,
Even when things are quite a fuss.
For in the dark, our dreams ignite,
With silly laughs that feel so right.

Luminous Whispers of the Night

The candles flicker on the table,
While stories weave, a night so fable.
A playful ghost, with sheet askew,
Claims he's the lost pet of our crew.

The hoot of owls sounds like laughter,
As shadows dance, endorsed by banter.
We sip our drinks, the ice cubes clink,
As thoughts are shared and spirits wink.

An alley cat joins in the fray,
Strutting like it's Broadway day.
With every step, the world's a stage,
In this bright weave, we're all the rage.

So let's embrace this starry cheer,
With giggles loud for all to hear.
For in this glow, we find our light,
With whispers turning into flight.

Dreams Adrift in Starlight's Hold

Beneath the glow of moonlit schemes,
Where wishes float on silly beams,
A cat with wings in disco shoes,
Dances with mice in vibrant hues.

A toaster sings a tune so sweet,
While socks engage in waltzing feet,
The clock ticks backward, laughs in jest,
As jelly beans become the quest.

Balloons sprout legs and take a jog,
While frogs wear hats and dance with dogs,
A night where dreams can't find their beds,
And giggles float above our heads.

So here we prance beneath the gleam,
In a world that's silly as a dream,
Where every star has something fun,
And laughter shines like morning sun.

The Enchantment of Hidden Radiance.

In midnight's glow, a skunk plays chess,
With fireflies trying to impress,
An owl in glasses writes a book,
While rabbits dance on golden mud.

A tuba frog jumps on a train,
Chasing after clouds of candy cane,
The wind plays tricks with silly hats,
As purring kittens plan their spats.

The stars begin a game of hide,
While playful ducks swim side by side,
A monkey juggles with a cake,
And giggles burst with every shake.

Here, laughter is the finest light,
That twinkles with the sheer delight,
In magic nights of whimsical play,
Where every moment finds a way.

Whispers Beneath the Stars

A penguin in a fancy hat,
Shares secrets with a curious cat,
While stars compose a vibrant tune,
That makes a sunflower sway and swoon.

A squirrel juggles acorns with flair,
As playful bears swing from the air,
The breeze tickles with cheeky laughs,
And jelly jars plan secret crafts.

Each twinkle hides a pearly joke,
That makes the fireflies fly and stoke,
With laughter wrapped in twilight's arms,
In whispered tones and funny charms.

So gather 'round, embrace the night,
Where silliness is pure delight,
Amongst the stars, we laugh and play,
In a delightful, quirky ballet.

Glimmers of Night's Embrace

In the frolic of a moonlit scene,
A bear plays chess with a limping queen,
While crickets chirp a serenade,
And sleepy goats in pajamas parade.

A dog strums chords on a gear-shaped harp,
Each note a giggle, each strum a lark,
While moths stage plays of great intent,
And fireworms create a colorful tent.

The night unfolds a game divine,
Where butterflies sip on fizzy wine,
And giggles float on cotton candy skies,
As gnomes wear crowns and jesters rise.

So dance beneath this starry gown,
Where laughter wears the brightest crown,
In every glimmer, a punchline waits,
With joy escaping through whimsical gates.

The Poetry of Nightfall Glimmers

Once the sun bids a silly adieu,
Stars peek out, and the moon joins a crew.
They chuckle and shimmer, a dance on high,
Whispering secrets in the velvet sky.

Street lamps flicker like disco balls on spree,
Cats strut like models, oh what a sight to see!
Neighbors stumble home, shoes in their hand,
Shadows play tag as they weave through the land.

A cricket's solo fills the park with delight,
While fireflies blink like they're texting at night.
Chasing the glow of a wayward burrito,
Humor's the currency, and laughter's the voto.

In this night circus, under stars, we glow,
Where every stumble and trip sparks a show.
So raise your glass high, let the fun take flight,
For every silly moment embroiders the night.

Veils of Radiance and Reminiscence

As twilight wraps in a quirky embrace,
Lights twinkle wildly, up lace and down grace.
Balloons float by with a giggle and sway,
Dancing with shadows, they join the ballet.

A city that snores turns alive with a tune,
And owls gossip softly under the moon.
Cars honk in rhythm, like a kooky parade,
While sleepy-eyed folks stumble, slightly dismayed.

Squirrels hold midnight snacks just like a feast,
Chasing their dreams, they're the nighttime least.
Laughter erupts from a late-night café,
Where dreams and desserts both frolic and play.

Each flicker of light tells a joke and a jest,
The night wears a grin, it's an unwritten quest.
With chocolate chip cookies and stories to share,
In this raucous night glow, nothing's quite rare.

Navigating Midnight's Glow

Navigating the night like ships on a brew,
Lost in the glow, where the odd becomes true.
A parade of odd socks, mismatched and bold,
Wanders the street as the tale is retold.

Moonbeams poke faces, awake like a tease,
With twirling lampposts that dance in the breeze.
Noses pressed on windows, curious eyes spy,
Aliens lounging while we try to fly.

A tune hums softly from somewhere obscure,
A saxophonist who thinks he's demure.
While sprightly raccoons hold a late-night chat,
Returning with bounty from rummaging rats.

And when all seems lost in a riddle of light,
We find laughter hiding, oh what a delight!
So trip through the alley of dreams and of cheer,
In this goofy glow, there's nothing to fear.

Threads of Light in the Stillness

Strands of gold weave through darkness so sly,
As laughter floats gently like whispers nearby.
Each light a giggle, a memory in flight,
That hugs us so warmly, as day turns to night.

Crackling voices spill stories like tea,
A bench holds the tales of your friend and me.
We stitch together the moments that gleam,
In the fabric of night, where we all chase a dream.

Windows aglow, like hearts full of mirth,
Each flicker's a smile, a joyful rebirth.
The night plays matchmaker with plans and delight,
As mischief and fun twinkle bright through the night.

So gather your buddies, no need to be shy,
For the threads of the evening are woven up high.
With laughter, we'll trellis the sweet things we find,
In this nighttime hush, let our spirits unwind.

Radiance of Underscored Twilight

Dancing cheese balls roll away,
In a party that has gone astray.
Laughter echoes through the night,
As friends trip over their own delight.

Balloons float higher than our hopes,
We juggle snacks and twisty ropes.
A cake that's leaning, a sight so sweet,
We cheer for crumbs under our feet.

Outrageous hats and goofy grins,
The night begins where chaos wins.
Under the glow of neon signs,
We sip our drinks and lose our minds.

As the clock strikes, we try to cheer,
An old dance craze brings us near.
With every joke, the laughter swells,
In this sweet mess, we find our spells.

Reflections on a Silver Canvas

A mirror ball spins, oh what a sight,
Reflecting antics, pure delight.
Socks on the floor, we take our stance,
In this chaos, we all dance!

Our reflections twist in humor's game,
As friends are lost, we call their name.
One shoe missing, a sock in hand,
We grab our snacks and make a stand.

The cookie jar is almost bare,
Who knew that dough would disappear?
Giggles echo, jokes on repeat,
In twilight's glow, we feel the beat.

With each reflection, our laughter grows,
These moments shine, that's how it goes.
With silver glimmers in every glance,
We weave the night in a funny dance.

Stars that Hide and Seek

Twinkling bulbs spark in quaint disguise,
While lost in hiding, we search the skies.
One giggles loud, another must shush,
Who's hiding where in this silly rush?

Behind the couch, we find old snacks,
Who knew they'd hide in such strange tracks?
Caught a glimpse of a friend's bright hair,
In this game, nothing seems unfair.

The dog thinks it's fun to join the chase,
As we tumble and fall all over the place.
Peeking past curtains, laughter runs free,
These silly stars light our victory.

In this dance of fun, we spark and streak,
With each surprise, we take a peek.
Who cares if we stumble, giggle, and fall?
In this light, we conquer it all!

Beneath the Electric Sky

Under bulbs that twinkle with glee,
Our gathering feels like a wild spree.
With sparklers igniting our silly fits,
We toast to life while laughing in bits.

The punch spills down, a colorful scene,
We dance around like we're on a screen.
Someone sings out of the tuneful way,
Yet here, we all cheer, not leading astray.

Strange snacks mix on our funky plates,
With every bite, we navigate fates.
Who knew broccoli could dance so fine?
In this odd menu, we all align.

Under the laughter of the glowing night,
We gather moments that feel so right.
With each funny story and jumbled cheer,
The electric sky brings us all near.

Radiance After Dark

In the night, the stars do wink,
While busy squirrels plot and think.
A raccoon in a top hat prances,
Chasing shadows as he dances.

The moon with cheese is up so high,
As owls spread their gossip sly.
Lights twinkle like they're on a spree,
While ants throw parties by the tree.

Jellybeans bounce on someone's head,
As fireflies twirl around in bed.
Laughter echoes through the air,
When a cat in pajamas declares, "I care!"

With every laugh, a glow appears,
As midnight snacks toast all their cheers.
The world, a game of hide and seek,
In the night, the silly feel unique.

Lamps of Longing and Wonder

A lamp can talk, or so they say,
It tells tales of yesterday.
With dreams of light, it grumbles loud,
While critters gather in a crowd.

The toadstool crew wears hats of red,
While giggling under the lamp's spread.
They ponder if the sun will frown,
Or if the stars will suit the town.

One little bug, confused and bold,
Announces it's time to be told.
"Do we follow the glow or roam?
I think I left my snacks at home!"

So bright they shine, these lamps of wonder,
Creating laughter, lifting thunder.
With every twist, they jig and sway,
Inviting all to dance and play.

Ballad of the Flickering Flame

A candle sings a wobbly tune,
With flames that dance beneath the moon.
The shadows twist, and oh, they prance,
As if they're caught in a glowing trance.

A moth in love with lights so bright,
Wears a bowtie for his big night.
He flutters round, both bold and spry,
As laughter echoes, oh my, oh my!

"Will you dance?" he shyly croons,
While hidden squirrels sing to tunes.
The candle's light, a playful spark,
Igniting wit within the dark.

So gather 'round, don't miss the show,
Where flickers lead our hearts to glow.
In every flick, a chance to play,
In laughter's warmth, we wish to stay.

Dreams Illuminated by Dusk

As twilight whispers, dreams take flight,
With shadows flitting left and right.
A jester plays a tune for fun,
While donuts roll, and smiles are spun.

The stars above begin to chatter,
While gnomes discuss who's fatter.
"Let's have a race to that old tree!"
Then off they go, quite joyfully.

With giggles loud, the night abounds,
As crickets cheer with merry sounds.
The moon becomes a giant pie,
And all the creatures start to sigh.

So let the dusk bring forth delight,
With every dream that takes its flight.
In laughter spun from twinkling cheer,
We find our magic, year by year.

Dreams Caught in Glimmering Threads

Beneath the sky's bright winks, they play,
A circus of dreams that sway and sway.
With laughter echoing in every direction,
Chasing fireflies, they seek the connection.

In a dance of hues, the children prance,
Twirling joyfully in a moonlit stance.
With ice cream mustaches, they spin around,
While giggles bounce like stars that astound.

A cat in a hat, looking quite bemused,
Watches the chaos, utterly confused.
While the night whispers secrets, tales of delight,
The world feels cozy, tilting just right.

So they twirl and tumble, embracing the night,
As sparkles linger, glowing in flight.
For in each glimmer, there's laughter to shed,
And dreams are the threads, in joy, they are fed.

Shadows Dancing with Light

Under the gaze of a streetlight's beam,
Shadows perform in a whimsical dream.
A waltz with the breeze on a sidewalk wide,
Their goofy movements, they can't seem to hide.

With a hop and a skip, they swirl and spin,
While old dogs chuckle, it's sure to begin.
A tap of the feet, it's a lively scene,
As everyone joins in, bursting with keen.

The lamp post nods like a wise old friend,
As shadows dip low, the giggles won't end.
Their mischief sparkles, a light-hearted feast,
In this nightly gala, tensions are ceased.

So they tease and they twine, those dark little forms,
Beneath the street's laughter, as magic transforms.
Moments like these fill the heart with such cheer,
Where shadows and light blend, year after year.

Stars Weaved into Urban Fabric

City lights twinkle, a blanket of glee,
As stars play peek-a-boo over rooftops free.
Weaving their stories in fabric of night,
Creating a canvas, oh what a sight!

A pigeon in glasses surveys the scene,
While mice in tuxedos dance like a dream.
With a wink to the moon, they take off in flight,
Turning the mundane into pure delight.

The sprinklers spray sparkles, a water ballet,
As laughter and chaos begin their foray.
Painting the sidewalks with giggles and cheers,
As the city sings songs that tickle the ears.

In neighborhoods bustling with joy and play,
Where every shadow has something to say.
These urban delights, we cherish so dear,
As stars weave their magic, bringing us cheer.

Pulses of Night's Gentle Heart

Under the glow of the moon's soft sigh,
The night's gentle pulse whispers 'Oh me, oh my.'
With crickets composing sweet symphonies profound,
Each note a chuckle that knows no bound.

A raccoon, with style, dons a fine vest,
Searching for snacks, he's a nocturnal guest.
In trash can theaters, with popcorn galore,
The audience gasps as he opens the door.

Fireflies flicker like quirky little lights,
Mapping the paths of the giggly nights.
As shadows play tag, with their comedic flair,
The laughter cascades, dissolving all care.

So let's raise a cheer to the nighttime brigade,
With whimsy and wonder, the memories made.
For within this dance of bright, silly sights,
The heart of the night is alive with delights!

Heartbeats of Glittering Darkness

Underneath the stars so bright,
Dancing fools lose all their might.
Laughter echoes through the night,
While cats in hats take flight!

Glitter on their shoes they wear,
Giant squirrels are in despair.
With popcorn hands, they share a dare,
As moonbeams pull the furry hair.

Now a tap dance, see it shine,
Hotdogs trade an ounce of wine.
A twinkling joke? It's quite divine,
But dancing with a fence? That's fine!

So lift your cups and toast with glee,
To all the joy that silly be!
In laughter's glow, we roam so free,
And every moment's pure jubilee!

Where Radiance Meets Silence

In the dark, a bulb can hum,
While squirrels ask, "Where's the rum?"
Glowing faces, all so numb,
Spinning tales with blissful drum.

Balloons that float, then start to dive,
Chasing shadows, does it thrive?
With giggles loud, and bees that jive,
This is where the fun's alive!

A cactus wears a neon hat,
Telling jokes to a sleepy rat.
The moon just sighed, perhaps it's fat,
While dancers waltz in loud purr chat.

Underneath this sparkling prism,
We dream of cats in wisdom's schism.
Take a seat, enjoy the rhythm,
As laughter breaks the still surrealism!

Echoes of the Neon Dream

Bright lights flash and colors twist,
Showcase of a funky list.
Dancing hedgehogs do insist,
To join the revelry, uncursed!

Under neon signs that frown,
A jester wears a silly crown.
Statues laugh, and tigers drown,
In sparkling waterfalls of brown.

With every step, the world does spin,
Giggly gremlins jump right in.
They turn around and flash a grin,
As ducks on roller skates begin!

So paint the night with laughter's hue,
Where even shadows dance and skew.
Join the fun, it's quite a view,
As echoes lead us to be true!

Twilight's Enchanted Glow

As twilight shimmers like a kiss,
A frog in glasses makes a bliss.
With each hop, there's laughter's hiss,
Whirling dreams in vivid mist.

Fireflies play a game of tag,
While owls drool from a snack bag.
With cupcakes fierce, they brag and wag,
As starlit gnomes untie the rag.

A chorus of lights, a jolly frog,
Croons to the beat of a dancing dog.
Underneath the shimmering smog,
Even shadows crack and clog.

Raise a toast to twilight's grace,
As laughter twirls in every space.
Let silliness lead every face,
In this magical, wobbling place!

The Hidden Beauty of Fading Stars

Once they danced with all their might,
Now they blink, it's quite the sight.
A cosmic wink, a cheeky show,
Lost their glow, but still say hello.

In pajamas, they shine so bright,
Yet trip on beams 'til dawn's first light.
Stars once proud with tales to share,
Now just giggle, 'Life's not fair!'

Their grand performance, a cosmic play,
Falling flat, as if to say:
'We're still here, come take a peek,
But please don't laugh; we are unique.'

With a flicker here and a twinkle there,
They just want to be debonair.
Fading gems in the night sky's fuss,
Whispering secrets, just for us.

Moonlit Whispers of Forgotten Dreams

Under the moon, dreams tend to sway,
Dancing lightly, they often stray.
Whispers of laughter, bobbing around,
A chorus of snores from the ground.

Once ambitious, now half asleep,
In twelve-hour talks about sheep.
'Oh to be young!' the moonlight sighs,
As it rolls its beams, these sleepy guys.

Lost aspirations, tucked away,
Slip on slippers, and go play.
Moonbeams scatter like confetti bold,
Faded hopes, daring but told.

With a chuckle, the stars poke fun,
At dreams abandoned, but still they run.
In night's embrace, all fears depart,
As laughter glows, a hopeful heart.

Flickers of Hope Above the Horizon

When daylight fades and darkness wakes,
A glint of laughter, that's what it takes.
Small fireflies don their party hats,
As crickets chirp silly chit-chat.

Up on the ledge, a flash unseen,
A lightbulb joke in between.
Flickers rise like a sneaky prank,
In a dance of lights, they laugh and prank.

Hope spills over, a comical spree,
Like a cat who thinks it's a tree.
With every flicker, the night inspires,
Chasing away those sleep-deprived fires.

So when the darkness bids us to hide,
Look for the giggles that coincide.
Laughing stars remind us to cope,
With each flicker, a promise of hope.

Night's Caress in a Sea of Lights

Nighttime blankets all with ease,
While lanterns chuckle and dance the breeze.
A sea of lights, so soft and round,
Shuffle together to make sweet sound.

With every glow, a giggle spills,
Pointing out the funny hills.
They play hide and seek in the dark,
While winking moons let out a spark.

This starlit banter, a nightly grind,
Where laughter echoes, blind to the blind.
Each light a giggle, a twinkle, a tease,
Making wishes on things that appease.

So let's toast to the shine of the night,
And wear our giggles all day bright.
For in this glow, fun finds its way,
In a dazzling outfit, we laugh and sway.

Beyond the Flicker of Forgotten Memories

Beneath the stars, I walked so tall,
Tripped on my shoelace, I soon took a fall.
Laughed at the moon, who giggled back bright,
As I danced with the shadows, under the night.

Whispers of laughter filled the cool air,
A squirrel on my shoulder, what a bizarre pair!
He offered me nuts, I politely declined,
He just winked at me, curious and blind.

The ghosts of my past threw a wild parade,
With balloons and confetti, a grand masquerade.
I joined in their dance, though I tripped on my feet,
The night turned to joy, can't accept defeat.

As dawn nudged the stars to take their own leave,
I laughed at the chaos, what do you believe?
Every blunder a gem, every slip quite divine,
In the flickers of fun, I couldn't help but shine.

A Glimpse of Brilliance Among Shadows

Under the glow of an unsteady lamp,
I found a lost sock, its color a stamp.
It grinned at me funny, with a hole in the toe,
"Wear me," it whispered, "you'd steal the show!"

Cackling shadows played tricks with my mind,
They mocked my great posture—I'm one of a kind!
In the silence, I shouted, "Who's there?" to the gloom,
An echo responded, "Your thoughts fill the room."

Illusions danced by with their whimsical flair,
A cat shaped like pizza leaped through the air.
I blinked, double-checked my sanity's clutch,
My friends laughed so hard, they lost it too much.

But within the absurd, a lesson seemed clear,
Life's slapstick moments bring joy, never fear.
So I shimmy with shadows, escape their embrace,
In the brilliance of laughter, I've found my true place.

Celestial Glows and Silent Thoughts

Stars were quite chatty when twilight arrived,
I threw out my wishes, they chuckled and thrived.
A comet zipped by, forgot its own trail,
With a wink and a shrug, like, 'Oops! Did I fail?'

The planets were busy, discussing their plight,
"Who'll be our host for this glorious night?"
Jupiter joked, "Let Saturn take lead,
He can spin up a ring, that's sure to succeed."

Meteors struggled, gave up on their speed,
"Chase after the moon? Nah, let it take the lead!"
I chimed in with giggles, "You twinkle too bright,
Let's embrace this oddness, enjoy this strange night!"

As laughter spread wide through the shimmering dome,
Each celestial body felt right at home.
With whispers of joy, we painted the skies,
In each silvery twinkle, a new laugh would rise.

When Darkness and Luminescence Embrace

In the murky depths where the dull shadows play,
I stumbled on bright fairies who'd lost their way.
With wings made of glitter and giggles so loud,
They twirled all around me, forming a crowd.

I tickled a shadow who shrieked with delight,
"Why hide in the dark? Come dance in the light!"
It stretched out its arms, turned luminous and bold,
And I laughed 'til my sides got chubby and cold.

The moon threw a party, invited the stars,
To toast with wild laughter from Venus to Mars.
I juggled two comets, dropped one in fright,
A crash in the cosmos, what a charming sight!

As darkness and brightness learned how to play,
With jokes in the air, my worries gave way.
Together we laughed, what a heavenly race,
In the dance of our quirks, we found our own space.

Luminescence and Lament

Beneath the glow, the cat did prance,
Chasing beams, it seized its chance.
A moth swooped low, a daring feat,
Poor kitty fell face-first, oh what a treat!

The moonlight giggled, with dazzling glee,
As socks and shoes danced with esprit.
A lost sock winked, I swear it did,
It sparked a party, beneath the lid!

But laughter echoed as light turned dim,
"Why so serious?" joked the bin.
The stars all snickered, shone bright and bold,
They plotted mischief, oh, tales untold!

So when you're lost in whims of night,
Embrace the chaos, let out a bite.
For every lament, there's a glimmering jest,
Life's funny dances put us to the test!

The Dance of Distant Stars

Stars waltzed wildly in velvet skies,
Pointing fingers, oh, what a surprise!
A couple tripped, fell on the ground,
Their laughter echoed, a joyous sound.

Neon lights flickered, a sign for fun,
As comets raced, just on the run.
A cosmic disco, spinning so bright,
Space boots tangled, what a sight!

Beneath a starlit, shimmering dome,
Aliens soared, calling it home.
They chuckled and twirled, just like a spree,
Galactic antics, so carefree!

Remember, dear friend, when the night sings,
Let go of worries, and spread your wings.
For every twinkle, a story's found,
Let laughter and light forever abound!

Secrets Wrapped in Luminous Glow

In a glow that feels like silly dreams,
The toaster hummed with giggly beams.
It popped up bread with a little cheer,
As crickets chuckled around us here.

The cookies danced on the kitchen rack,
While shadows whispered, "Hey, look back!"
An oven mitt waved, oh what a presage,
"Join the fun!" it said with a message.

Wrapped in laughs, the world's a jest,
Where even a sandwich may take a rest.
So toast your dreams under fluorescent skies,
For secrets sparkle where laughter lies!

Night's curtain drops, the stars won't wait,
Embrace the mismatch, and celebrate!
For each hidden giggle, under the moon's show,
There's joy in every luminous glow!

Celestial Murmurs Between Realms

Whispers travel through stellar streams,
The universe chuckles, bursting at seams.
A comet hiccupped, its tail in flight,
While planets shimmied, oh, what a sight!

The sun grinned wide, with a cheeky glare,
"Let's prank that black hole, just for flair!"
While galaxies twirled in a dizzying dance,
Creating a spectacle, ignite a chance!

Planets disciplined, spun in their lanes,
Yet a rogue moon skipped, ignoring the chains.
Stars exchanged glances, a timeless jest,
"Let's stir some trouble, for fun, not rest!"

So lift your head, let laughter ring,
For cosmic capers make souls take wing.
In murmurs of starlight, the worlds entwine,
Embrace the chaos, let spirits shine!

Glistening Veils of Night

In the twilight's funny grin,
Stars are winking, let's begin.
A cat walks on a fence so high,
Chasing dreams and butterflies.

Balloons are floating, dancing free,
A squirrel swings from tree to tree.
The moon's a pie, round and bright,
Making everyone feel light.

With shadows playing hide and seek,
The crickets chirp a tune so cheek.
A silly dance, a tip of hat,
Even a wise old owl's a brat.

So join the laugh under the sky,
Where giggles rise and troubles fly.
The night's alive with playful glee,
A circus show for you and me.

Beneath the Cosmic Glimmer

Underneath the sparkling dome,
We wander far away from home.
The stars are chuckling, what a sight,
They play hide and seek at night.

With pizza slices tossed so high,
A comet zooms on by, oh my!
A dancing dog with floppy ears,
Steals the show and brings us cheers.

Galaxies giggle in delight,
As we trip and fall, oh what a night!
The planets join a conga line,
Making mischief, feeling fine.

So hold my hand, let's swirl around,
With laughter echoing all around.
When cosmic winds begin to sway,
We'll chase our troubles far away.

Whispering Echoes of Dusk

As day bows low with a sigh of glee,
The squirrels plan a grand jubilee.
A rustle here, a plop over there,
A wise old turtle's in mid-air.

The evening hums a silly tune,
While frogs croak backup, oh what a boon!
The fireflies flash like disco lights,
Inviting all to funny fights.

A shadow plays the ukulele,
While beetles march like a ballet.
With giggles popping like balloons,
We dance away beneath the moons.

So let the night wear its playful hat,
With every twinkle, let's have a chat.
Laughter weaves through each soft breeze,
Tickling our hearts with gentle ease.

Flickering Dreams in Starlight

The stars are twirling in a race,
While comets wear a funny face.
The wishes float on cotton candy,
A silly dreamer, always dandy.

With whipped cream clouds that bounce and play,
A jellybean sky that's here to stay.
The laughter echoes through the night,
With every bounce, we touch new heights.

The moon juggles dreams with flair,
As wishes twinkle in the air.
Giggles rise like bubbles in tune,
A waltz beneath the watching moon.

So let us dance, just you and me,
In this space of pure jubilee.
With every flicker, let's rejoice,
And give the universe a voice.

Echoes of Light's Hidden Stories

Beneath the brightness, secrets hide,
A dance of shadows, side by side.
The moon winks at the stars so bright,
While crickets share their jokes of night.

A cat in shades with glasses on,
Stares at the sky till the break of dawn.
He laughs at clouds that float with glee,
What a silly sight, oh can't you see?

The streetlamps gossip, tales unfold,
Of lost socks and stories retold.
They flicker with laughter, a glow they bring,
Like comedic actors, they dance and sing.

So gather close, let the fun ignite,
Where shadows whisper under the light.
In this odd world where mischief roams,
Even streetlights call the night their home.

Wisps of Light Against the Dark

Glowing wisps in the evening air,
Bumblebees buzzing without a care.
The moon lost its hat, it's just a joke,
As fireflies dodge a haphazard poke.

Dancing shadows play hide and seek,
A sock puppet gets a little cheek.
Crickets in tuxedos chirp with flair,
While beetles strut in the cool night air.

A picnic gone wrong, with ants on a spree,
Stealing crumbs as funny as can be.
Laughter erupts where the starlights beam,
All under the glow of a silvery dream.

Whispers of fun in the chilled night sky,
Secrets of silliness that twinkle and fly.
In this bright realm where mischief is sparked,
Even the night seems a bit off-mark.

Mysteries Wrapped in Glow

Beneath the lantern's flickering gaze,
Lurks a mystery that prompts a haze.
A rubber chicken lays still by the pine,
Where owls peer down, sharing jokes divine.

A squirrel with shades, he struts with pride,
Sketching dreams in the open wide.
As bugs wear tuxes for their night ballet,
Who knew a glow could be such a play?

Comets fly past with a giggling sound,
While shadows dispute who's the funniest around.
Each dark corner holds a curious laugh,
As lanterns gossip on a whimsical path.

So join in the fun, let laughter alight,
Where mysteries shimmer and wiggle at night.
In a world where giggles fill the air,
Even the stars seem to dance and care.

Flickering Conversations with the Night

Quietly glimmering, the stars start to play,
As night-time chatters in a humorous way.
A moonlit caper where owls take the stage,
Their punchlines echo from page to page.

The shadows twist in a dramatic jest,
Brightly lit tales invite the rest.
With sneakers on, the trees start to rock,
And bushes chuckle, inspired by a clock.

A firefly agent with a badge so bright,
Turns on the charm to solve the night's plight.
Each giggle bounces, each chuckle glows,
Beneath a sky where the laughter flows.

So listen up close, hear the night's cheer,
In each flickering laugh, find warmth so near.
In this realm where comedy's the guide,
Every shimmer echoes the fun inside.

Milton Keynes UK
Ingram Content Group UK Ltd.
UKHW030749121124
451094UK00013B/837

9 789916 943816